Lightning Bolt Books™

Weather Robots

Christine Zuchora-Walske

Lerner Publications

Minneapolis

Lerner Publications Company
A division of Lerner Publishing Group, Inc.
241 First Avenue North
Minneapolis, MN 55401 USA

For reading levels and more information, look up this title at www.lernerbooks.com.

Cover photo: The Aeryon Scout gathers weather information and sends real-time videos of the weather conditions to its pilot on the ground.

Library of Congress Cataloging-in-Publication Data

The Cataloging-in-Publication Data for Weather Robots is on file at the Library of Congress.
ISBN 978-1-4677-4057-9 (LB)
ISBN 978-1-4677-4693-9 (EB pdf)

Manufactured in the United States of America
2 — BP — 9/1/15

Table of Contents

What Is a Robot? — page 4

Flying Robots — page 10

Swimming Robots — page 16

Driving Robots — page 22

Robot Scientists — page 28

Fun Facts — page 29

Glossary — page 30

Further Reading — page 31

Index — page 32

What Is a Robot?

Robots are machines that do work. They use sensors to learn about the world around them.

ROV
KIEL 6000

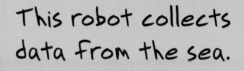
This robot collects data from the sea.

Weather robots collect data about our environment. Some help predict weather.

Some weather robots use sensors to measure wind speed. **Others use sensors to measure temperature.**

Large robots can carry many sensors at once.

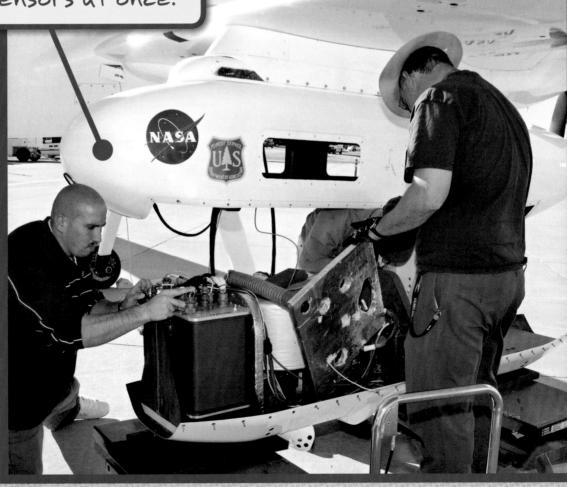

Weather robots fly, swim, and drive. They need energy to move. This energy can come from gas or batteries. Or it can come from sunlight or wind.

A robot needs a brain. Its brain is a computer. The computer contains a program. Programs tell robots what to do. Climate scientists create programs.

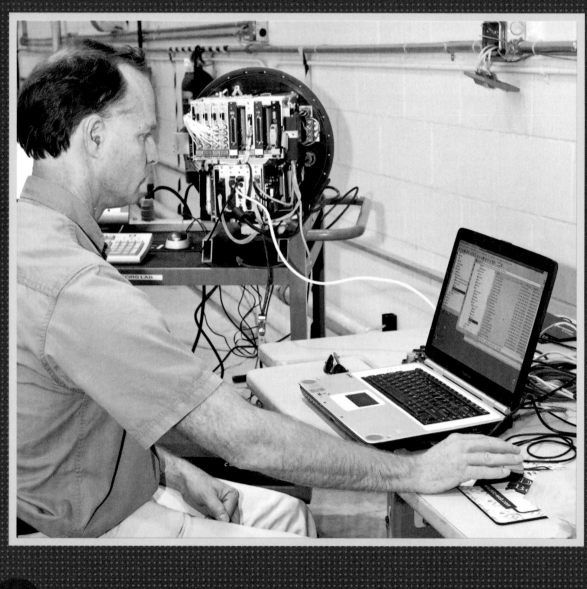

Weather robots help us understand weather. They also help us study climate change.

Scientists use data from robots to help predict storms.

Flying Robots

Some weather robots fly. They are called UAVs. UAVs are small airplanes or helicopters.

IKHANA

NASA

Pilots and scientists control UAVs and read data from the ground.

UAVs do not carry people. They carry only sensors. Some of these measure temperature. Others measure wind and humidity.

Flying into storms is dangerous. But some UAVs can fly in rough weather. They gather data. Scientists study this data. They learn how storms form.

Small, tough UAVs can survive storms.

This UAV carries sensors under its left wing.

UAVs are very useful for studying storms. Ground sensors measure only what passes above them. But UAVs can follow storms.

Strong winds and rain don't
stop these robots.

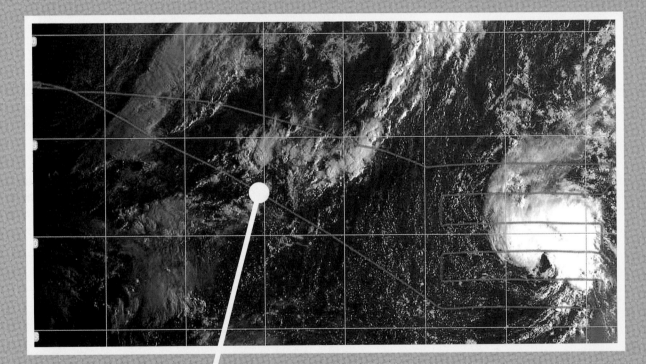

This red line shows
the path of a UAV
through a hurricane.

Scientists program
some UAVs to fly
like bees.

Some robots can
fly like insects.

Bees fly well in bad weather.
They fly slowly. They roll
often. This keeps them stable
in high winds.

Swimming Robots

Some weather robots swim.
They record ocean currents.

Ocean currents carry heat.
They affect weather around
the planet.

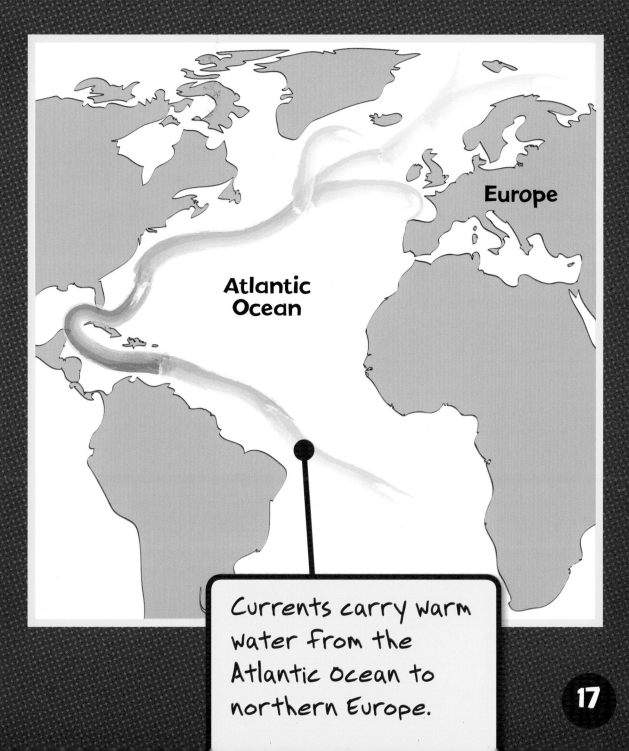

Europe

Atlantic
Ocean

Currents carry warm
water from the
Atlantic Ocean to
northern Europe.

This robot rises
and sinks in place
to collect data
from the ocean.

Some ocean robots float in place.
They measure temperature and
salinity. Salinity is the saltiness
of water.

Other ocean robots chase hurricanes!

Hurricanes are so big they can be seen from space.

Some robots chase hurricanes under water. They swim toward the storm. They help scientists predict where hurricanes will go.

Robots called gliders travel under water.

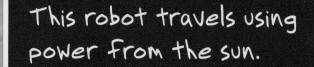

This robot travels using power from the sun.

Other robots stay on the surface. They carry sensors into the middle of hurricanes.

Driving Robots

Some weather robots drive on land. They explore harsh places. They send scientists data about weather.

This robot explores weather on ice sheets in Greenland.

Volcanoes can change the weather.
They create dust clouds. These
clouds block sunlight. Without
sunlight, Earth cools.
The cold can last for
months or years.
Robots can
warn scientists
about eruptions.

Volcano robots roll on wheels or walk on legs. They travel into volcanoes. They sense temperatures and gases. Scientists study this data to predict eruptions.

Wheeled robots map Antarctica.
They take ice and snow samples.
They sense temperature, wind,
and snowfall.

These robots
look like small
snowmobiles.

Earth's climate is warming. Polar ice is melting. Melting ice changes ocean currents.

Scientists place robots in the oceans to predict the weather.

Weather robots study the North and South Poles. Robots help scientists track Earth's warming. Robots can predict climate changes. Their data helps us prepare for the future.

Robot Scientists

- Robot scientists are called roboticists. To become a roboticist, you must go to college for at least four years.

- Creating robots involves engineering, math, and computer programming. To work with weather robots, you must also understand meteorology. This is the science of weather.

- Weather robots must be able to survive harsh weather. The people who build weather robots must think about how they will move in high winds or large waves.

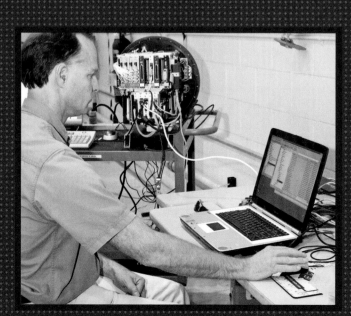

Fun Facts

- Some ocean robots get energy from ocean waves. Polar robots get energy from wind and the sun.

- One ocean robot project includes about three thousand robots floating across the world's oceans. The project began in 1999. By November 2012, the robots had collected more than one million readings.

- One volcanic robot has eight legs, like a spider. The robot creeps around a volcano's crater. The robot looks for fumaroles, or cracks spewing superhot gases. The robot stands over the cracks for hours and collects data.

- The US National Weather Service's weather radio broadcasts are gathered, organized, and broadcast by a robot.

Glossary

climate: usual weather patterns over time

current: a river of moving water within the ocean

data: information

eruption: when dust, ash, gas, and lava burst out of a volcano

humidity: moisture in the air

hurricane: a giant storm with high winds and heavy rains. Hurricanes form over warm oceans.

predict: to say what will happen in the future

program: a set of computer instructions

robot: a machine that does work for humans. A robot must be able to move and sense the world around it.

salinity: the amount of salt in water

UAV: unmanned aerial vehicle. UAVs carry sensors but no passengers.

Further Reading

Ceceri, Kathy. *Robotics: Discover the Science and Technology of the Future with Twenty Projects.* White River Junction, VT: Nomad Press, 2012.

Domaine, Helena. *Robotics.* Minneapolis: Lerner Publications, 2006.

Galileo Educational Network: Robotics
http://www.galileo.org/robotics

Idaho Public Television Dialogue for Kids: Robots
http://idahoptv.org/dialogue4kids/season10/robots

Kops, Deborah. *Exploring Space Robots.* Minneapolis: Lerner Publications, 2012.

NASA Robots Storybook
http://www.nasa.gov/audience/forstudents/k-4/stories/ames-robot-storybook-text.html

Stewart, Melissa. *Robots.* Washington, DC: National Geographic Children's Books, 2014.

Tech Museum: Robotics
http://www.thetech.org/exhibits/online/robotics

Index

Antarctica, 25

climate, 8, 9, 26, 27
computers, 8
currents, 16, 17, 26

data, 5, 12, 22, 24, 27

environment, 5

hurricanes, 14, 19, 20, 21

ice, 25, 26

salinity, 18
scientists, 8, 12, 15, 20, 22, 23, 24, 27
sensors, 4, 6, 11, 13, 21
storms, 12, 13, 20

temperature, 6, 11, 18, 24, 25

UAVs, 10, 11, 12, 13, 14, 15

volcanoes, 24

Photo Acknowledgments

The images in this book are used with the permission of: © Festo/Rex Features/AP Images, pp. 2, 15; © Baloncici/Shutterstock Images, p. 4; © Carsten Rehder/picture-alliance/dpa/AP Images, p. 5; NASA, pp. 6, 8, 10, 11, 13, 14, 18, 19, 22, 28, 30; © Stephane Bidouze/Shutterstock Images, p. 7; © Alan Diaz/AP Images, p. 9; © Oklahoma State University, Gary Lawson/AP Images, p. 12; © Handout/Reuters/Corbis, p. 16; © kaarsten/Shutterstock Images, p. 17; © Robert Sciarrino/The Star-Ledger/Corbis, p. 20; © PRNewsFoto/Savannah Ocean Exchange/AP Images, p. 21; © wdeon/Shutterstock Images, p. 23; © Bill Ingalls/Time & Life Pictures/Getty Images, p. 24; © Georgia Tech, Ron Felt/AP Images, p. 25; © Curioso/Shutterstock Images, p. 26; © CSIRO/AP Images, pp. 27, 31.

Front Cover: © Aeryon Labs, Inc.

Main body text set in Johann Light 30/36.